T0210056

EARTH
AND
WATER

A.S THOMAS

authorHOUSE®

AuthorHouse™
1663 Liberty Drive
Bloomington, IN 47403
www.authorhouse.com
Phone: 1 (800) 839-8640

Published by AuthorHouse   02/12/2019

ISBN: 978-1-5462-7966-2 (sc)
ISBN: 978-1-5462-7965-5 (e)

Library of Congress Control Number: 2019901484

Print information available on the last page.

DEDICATION

I dedicate this book to my loving husband and legendary son, my phenomenal family, fantastic friends, and anyone who inspired me or helped me along the journey here on Earth. Thank you, God. Universe. Mother Nature.

PROLOGUE

Sanni the tsunami
goes on a journey
she is a wave
flowing high and low
making her way here on earth
don't waste too much time
trying to make sense of these rhymes
these are thoughts
there's no right or wrong
just go along.

I want to be like water, a force without
boundaries, free and flowing, and
an impact to everything.

She was free as the ocean breeze
tall like the island trees
cool like the water stream
every man desired her company
and craved her badly
she was deserving and worthy
she was God's property
she was so earthly
her eyes were so dreamy
her hair was kinky
her smile was flirty
she spoke so eloquently
she walked so fiercely
she moved so vibrantly
she did things tastefully
she dressed classy
little things made her happy
but her attitude was feisty
her wrath felt like the tsunami
her name is Sanni.

You are the sum of all your
choices said a wise man
and I am
never will I feel sorry for being
born a black african
it is my unique story that will rise me to glory
for I am not ashamed of the
choices I have made
I have been through pain
and cried with the sky rain
depressed confined to my
demons, trapped in a cage
I didn't see the light nor day
but the darkness didn't prevail
I had to cure myself and go away
one by one
each tragedy
I overcame
now my faith still remains
I am guilty of a crime and sin
for actions that should have never been
the worst thing I've ever done to myself
was not believe in myself
because I didn't love myself
I was too busy trying to change myself
instead of embracing myself
so I told myself
you've got to love yourself
be patient with yourself
redeem yourself
find yourself

know yourself
believe in yourself
help yourself
humble yourself
be yourself
because
you are made of magic and tragedies
gold and alchemy
pain and agony
fantasy and harmony
I am a fleeting melody
filled with positivity
most days I'm up
some days I'm down
still I always remember to wear my crown
I am not perfect
but I've got a purpose
I have an image to portray
a message to convey
masses to inspire
thousands to admire
millions to lead
goals to achieve
I've got to get the people to believe
and I won't stop
until my heart dies and my body drops
and even when I die
my soul will always fly high
my legacy will live on forever
I'll always be known as the people's defender
passionate writer
amazing storyteller
kind hearted woman and selfless giver
because I am queen
Queen Sanni

God's property
deserving and worthy
so God damn earthly
all because of the choices
I, God, and nature destined for my life journey.

Higher vibrations leading me to higher learning and higher purpose.

I have no desire to be liked or
understood, rather to be felt
if I leave you feeling a part of my love, part
of my energy, or reality, I have succeeded
popularity fades but feelings last a lifetime.

Substance over popularity.

Please understand that it doesn't
matter who wishes you the best
If God ordains it you are destined for success.

I am a writer, writing from my
heart, all ways, always
I write what I feel, what I think,
and when I cannot speak
I write because I have too much
souls for assholes and hoes who
can't hold a verbal convo
I write because what some teachers,
preachers, and world leaders advocate doesn't
always resonate with my consciousness
I write to discover
I write to uncover what lies in my spirit and soul
I write even when people continue
to judge a book by its cover
I write because I can
I write because it's a part of me
I write for freedom
I write for strength
I write for guidance
I write for my loved ones and my community
I write to make up for lost time
I write because it keeps me going
I write and write and will continue to
write until my heart gives out
I write about what eyes cannot see
where feet cannot run,
what hands cannot touch, and
what ears cannot hear
still I write
because I can
because its apart of me
I write to the beat
I write to the sound of the breeze, wind, and sea
I write late at night with the stars and moon
I write until the sun rises
I write to God

I write because of my faith
I write because I'm grateful
I write to manifest my words into action
I write to inspire
I write to represent
I write to achieve
I write to bring about change
I write because my words are my
tools of weapon and magic
I write to create
I write because I can and
because its apart of me
I write when no one gets me
I write when I can't understand my emotions
I write for clarity
I write to tranquility and serenity
I write because it makes me happy
I write because it's my second nature
I write because its love
I write for peace, a peace of mind,
and peace worldwide
I write whatever, whenever,
however, about whoever
I write because there are poems inside of me
that only pen and paper can comprehend
I write because it's a gift
I write because my words are my power
I write because I can, because its apart of me
I write because its an emotional art
that comes from the heart.

I just want to write all day and dress like
I'm supposed to be on the runway
but I've got goals to accomplish baby.

Write away your worries
sleep away your pain
cry away your sorrows
kiss away your mistakes
and hug tomorrow
because everything is going to be okay.

Don't let our ideas go to waste
create.

Let your heart be your religion
break yourself out of mental prison
be who you are even if you are criticized
then watch your blessings become magnified.

Believe in yourself and let faith remain
trust yourself and let happiness pervade
do what your heart desires and
never be ashamed
you have the right not to explain
you have the right to exclaim
you have the right to be untamed
you are the master of your fate
don't let your doubts invade
don't wait a day longer and procrastinate
free yourself
don't let your soul parade in vein
let go of fear,
shout it out and proclaim
proclaim your happiness!

Your love is mandatory
your happiness is compulsory
your peace is necessary.

When you are feeling down and grey
always remember cloudy days fade away.

Three months was all it took
in three months, my love for you only grew
in three months, I knew I was meant for you
in three months, I'm ready to say I do
in three months, my heart now belongs to you
my mind body and soul too.

I know love
I mean real love
love that you pray for
love that you go to bed wishing on a star for
love that is infinite and limitless
love that has no boundaries
love that makes you do things you
never thought you could
love that makes you know nothing is impossible
love that makes your faith stronger
love that makes your fears a thing of the past
love that you didn't even know could exist
love that gets you higher than drugs
love that makes you love everything
I thank God for this type of love.

Your love lingers on my skin
your passion breathes on my neck
your kisses caress my senses
your touch melts my heart
your love captures my soul
your eyes gazes at my spirit
your joy is my joy
your happiness infiltrates my mind
your tongue takes me to places
I never knew existed
your presence makes me feel
things that I can only imagine
your fragrance is something I always envision,
light free strong and contagious
twenty-four hours with you feels like a lifetime
you slow down time with just your energy
you give me really deep vibes
you take me to my climax
you go deep into my walls and explore with in
each stroke is a magical sin
I take control and I climb to the throne
just five seconds on top and I make you moan
I am a queen and you are my king
I let you know that this is yours and yours to own
you never have to feel alone
I pull you close
our bodies collide and our souls unite
your love is now my appetite
I desire you all of the time and all of the excite
the penetration and the explosion
when it's all over I release all of my emotions
lying next to you motionless.

Because of him
God is in her walk
God is in her heart
God is in her smile
God is in her scent
the galaxy is in her eyes
and the universe is a part of her
a legend was conceived and lived inside her
she gave birth and now the
legend lives with her.

Mr. O
let's envision the scenario
you're visible, I'm incognito
sitting and listening to the radio
I call your name and tell you
that I need you pronto
you listen, then follow
as you walk closer
you view my silhouette and shadow
you walk in the room and I give you a freak show
instantly you become aroused
as I galvanize you rip off my blouse
you pull me in close to your chest
then you lay me down to rest
you kiss my neck and suck my breast
now I'm wet
I rub my hands on your head
then you moan
and I'm blown
I suck your neck and taste your cologne
you whisper in my ears and say
my body is yours to explore
my body roars
I tell you give me more
I want you
I yearn for you
physically, mentally, and emotionally
I need you to be a part of me
all of you and all of the time,
you're always on my mind
I'm so glad your mine
I can't help but smile.

Loving me will break you into pieces
and build you back up concurrently
loving me is not easy
I desire love to revolve around me
yet have a hard time letting it circulate freely
I am a fleeting melody most days
I'm up some days I'm down
I am selfish and self-centered
I can be a walk in the park on a sunny
afternoon or a marathon around the park
circling over and over in the same routine
loving me is deeper than abyss
loving me is true strength and courage
loving me is so complicated
loving me is a test of patience
loving me forms a thin line
between love and hate
loving me is a mix of blissfulness and heartache
loving me is stressful
loving me is joyful
loving me is plentiful
loving me is teaching me
loving me is showing me
loving me is caring for me
loving me is pushing me
loving me is accepting me
loving me is compromising for me
loving me is praying for me
loving me is sharing with me
loving me is crying with me
loving me is yelling at me
loving me is getting upset or frustrated
because of the strong love you have for me
loving me hurts
loving me is tiring
loving me is irreplaceable

loving me is being faithful
loving me is virtuous
loving me is God's work
loving me is loyalty
loving me is risky
loving me is energy in motion going
through every emotion
but loving you my dear is the greatest lesson
and self-reflection of my heart truet desires
loving you makes me want to be better
loving you motivates me
loving you fortifies me
loving you makes me happy
loving you is surreal
loving you is a journey
loving you is accepting you
loving you is learning from you
loving you is trial and error
loving you is a tribulation
loving you is forgiving
loving you is authentic
loving you diminishes my insecurities
loving you is a dependency
loving you is a satisfaction
loving you is challenging
loving you is continuous
loving you is loving myself
loving you is saying I'm sorry
loving you is never being able to pay you
back for all that you've done for me but
being internally and forever grateful
loving you has been one of the
greatest experiences of my life
loving you is like oxygen, necessary.

I didn't mean to
I didn't want to
I've got to make things right
I made him cry himself to bed at night
I took away his will and might
I was supposed to be his anchor
but instead I filled him with anger
I hurt him bad
I got him mad
I made him vulnerable and weak
Like a thief in the night
I left him wide open
destroyed his most inner happiness
till it ached his bones
damn it! I got the blues and I'm feeling low
how can he ever trust me again?
lord knows I don't want this love to end
he's my kin
the yin to my yang
the g to our gang
strength
I'll say it again
strength
It's all that I need
to fill him up again
bring him up again
restore his faith and make him believe again
when he is hurt I am hurt
when he is down I am down
he is a part of me just as much I am a part of him
when I hurt him I hurt myself
he's always been more than I'll never need
silly me
foolish me
selfish me
he's the air that I breathe

he's my oxygen, his love fills me up
without it I am incomplete
when I look in his eyes
he takes me out of this world
and gives me a high
I owe it all to him
for I am woman
a strong woman
honored in loved and dipped in faith
and I'll do anything to make him fly
when it's all said and done
we'll soar high together like birds in the sky.

Darling, if I gave you all of my soul
you wouldn't know how to cope.

I am completely okay with being alone
sometimes you've got to learn to check
your frequencies and take note
find out what is good and bad for your soul.

Music is more than just music
music is like going on a cruise through
every emotion and at each stop the
beat lets out a different vibe
music is like being in an ocean of waves
and you either drown in it or float with it
music is what guides
music is a universal language
music isn't prejudice, it doesn't
discriminate, and it has no race
music is man's greatest advantage
music is education, a manifestation
and a way of communication
music teaches about life on earth
while giving people the power
to know their worth
music is more than a voice
music is so much more than just loud noise
in fact music is so extraordinary that it
should be played out loud or not at all
music cannot be boxed, it has
no boundaries, or walls
music is a production of melody base
tempo cadence pitch and notes
music is multiple sounds coming together
creating something spectacular
music is freedom
music is a kingdom
music is an experience
music is more than a beat
music is an expression of how I feel
music is what I use to heal
music is my drug of choice
when I'm full of sorrow
music gives me hope for a better tomorrow
music is the common denominator

music is what unites people and
brings them together
music creates an everlasting
impact on countless hearts
music is an emotional art
music is the rhythm of life and life of the party
music is used to entertain and inspire
music is what ignites my inner fire
music takes me to my peak
when I am feeling weak
when I need to be alone, I
unplug myself from society
plug in my headphones,
just to regain my sanity
music is how I cope in time of need
How could music ever become obsolete?
music is forever
music is highly favored
music is what I truly adore
music makes my soul and spirit soar
music is so GOD DANM spiritual
I remember being seven and begging
my dad for a portable CD player
I've never yearned for or wanted anything more
I thank God for weekends my dad
would use music to begin the day
The music genre ranged
Some of the artists were Fela
Kuti and King Sunny Ade
Angelique Kidjo, Salif Keita, Yousso
N'dor Ebeneezer Obey
Peter Tosh, Ub40, Bob Marley and The Wailers
Phil Collins, Slash, and Marvin Gaye
2pac, Snoop Dogg, and Dr.Dre.
Puff Daddy, Biggie, and Mase
Chaka Khan, Anita Baker, and Sade

Eminem, 50 cent, Ludarcris, and T.I
Whitney Houston, Michael Jackson,
Mariah Carey, and Toni Braxton
The Fugees, Nas, Jay-z and Janet Jackson
Madonna, Ricky Martin, Selena, and Celine Dion
this is how music became my ultimate getaway
now my heart resides in its landscape
music is love
if love is what makes the world go round,
music is the gravity that keeps it
from touching the ground
music is an institution, an attribution,
a distribution, and an evolution
music is the solution.

After every storm, just before the sun
comes out the rainbow forms
giving the world various hues
and splendid views
beautiful magnificent colors
toned, classic, and primary colors
a mixture of so many beautiful colors
an array of diverse wavy and bountiful colors
pattern, shapes, and monochromes
living life in color
people of color
it's time to come together
time to own our mixtures of color
the world is your run way
your time to strut and slay
be bold and shine bright
I know you ain't afraid to express yourself
I know you've been waiting to free
yourself and be yourself
the rules and standards of the
world or can't define you
don't be afraid to create the life
you've always dreamed about
like the rainbow filled with colors
it's time to feel and live life in color.

It's only been a year
and I'm so grateful to be here
the only thing holding me back is fear
I can't let it cripple me anymore
I can't be complacent any longer
how can I expect to be stronger?
I've got to leave this comfort zone
I've got to find a new abode
I'm leaving home.

My soul wants to roam
I want to dance in the sun
and have endless fun
I belong in the Caribbean
where my spirt can run free
I'm trying so hard to keep balance
at times I'm up other times I'm down
I'm so afraid to drown
I'm practicing daily so that I don't
I know in due time I'll be able to float.

She conceals her accent
to mask her origin of decent
when she left home, she was
sure she would represent
but when she came abroad, she was tormented
she conceals her accent
because of the many hardships she underwent
She conceals her accent
so she will no longer feel saddened
she never imagined being outcasted
because of her accent
she didn't want to believe this could happen
she conceals her accent not
because she is ashamed
but because she has to assimilate
in order to ascend and transcend
in a foreign man land
she conceals her accent as a part of a plan
to make herself hundreds of grands
she conceals here accent because
each time she speaks she is critiqued
when she reveals her true accent, they attempt
to belittle her and make her feel weak
she doesn't sound like them so
they turn the left cheek
instead of understanding that she is unique
they won't listen to her yet they make fun of her
she becomes outraged filled
with agitation and anger
they have no respect for her whatsoever
and because they can't comprehend her
they constantly interrogate her
making her feel like an incriminator
when they are the true wrongdoers
so she begins to emulate their ways
until she elevates

they no longer discriminate
all because she changed the
way she enunciates.

Do I turn the blind eye
or do I fight for what is right
when the flame within me ignites?
what must I do to get people to unite?
I tell myself I'll expedite a plan tonight
tonight turns into tomorrow,
which then becomes next week,
next month, and next year
a whole three hundred and
sixty-five days passes
and the vision of my mission is now unclear
it's a cyclical process that not only I but
so many of my peers adhere to
it's bigger than a race issue
humanity is becoming devalued
look at what media has done
they have captured our souls
belittled us, made fun of us, shunned
us and now they have won
I've tried so hard to escape these harsh realities
but the truth of the matter is I can't run
so I ask myself again
do I confide to the system stunts
to acquire my riches?
or do I follow my intuition,
fight for what is right, to be left with none.

Everything in life takes time
before I would look at the naked
stems and become impatient
I wanted to see more and became
so fixated on the end result
then it rained for what felt like forever
finally, the flower blossomed
when I least expected it
I thank God for the storm and rain
the growth and pain
and most especially the
beautiful transformation.

Style and grace,
beauty and brains,
it's not easily obtained,
yet she keeps it maintained
she's made the sky her domain
surpassing all constraints
a limit?
let's admit she doesn't have one
and each time you think she's done,
she's plotting for something as big as the sun
she's a creation of God, a wife to one,
a mother, a companion to some,
and a blessing to all
her generosity will leave you in awe
with a personality so electric
and a love so magnetic,
style so eccentric
and loyalty so authentic
it's no wonder she remains optimistic
her passion to educate is so great
she strives to help those behind her to elevate
her passion to be the best reaches
as far as the horizon
she has reached her pinnacle, made
everyone proud, and won
who is this phenomenal woman I speak of?

Little by little things happen, never give up.

This winter I saw a leaf grow
it was surrounded by so much snow
who would've known
in the cold, trees could grow.

You may doubt my every existence
and divine purpose
but I am stronger than you think
does my presence make you nervous
because I am stronger than you think?
you may try to control me, break, or fold me
but I am stronger than you think
does my strength come as a surprise?
are you frightened because I am wise?
a spirit of good vibes
able to overcome any demise and rise
you may lie, criticize, antagonize,
and scrutinize me
but I am stronger that you think
I radiate positivity
smile excessively
laugh outrageously
and live happily
why does it make you feel shamefully?
is it because I live free and courageously?
did you want to see me quit?
It crossed my mind, I must admit
but I am stronger than you think.

I might bend but I will not break.

Why is media such a distraction?
why is the news such a contradiction?
why does stories about celebrities
cause grand reactions?
Why does this bring the audience satisfaction?
how come majority of society doesn't
know advertisements are put in
place to make transactions?
why did twitter, instagram, and facebook
become a form of social interaction?
why does certain stories make headlines?
while other stories are undermined
could it be a way to keep citizens aligned?
perhaps it's the way media defines
and design what news is assigned
to make citizens feel inclined
how much money does a show like super
bowl Sunday make large corporations?
if a CEO of one, makes a dollar for
each person's participation
multiply that by just a million viewers
so now tell me who are the wrongdoers?
the corporations or the citizens of the nation?
maybe there isn't a valid accusation
has the formation of media been
like this since its foundation?
was media created to keep citizens
aware and educated?
or was it really put in place to propagate?
what's the correlation between
communication and cultivation?
could it be information and domination?
how does someone have so much power
to keep the population so fascinated?
to the point that citizens are paying
for such entertainment

Is it not by the virtue of the participation
and compensation of citizens
that enable entertainers, producers,
and CEO's to have occupations?
the creation of media must've
been highly orchestrated
its presentation, publication, reformation, and
variation all make it a unique application
I just wonder how many regulations
are put in place to conceal its daily
and continuous moral violations.

I stopped believing in coincidences
a long time ago
now all of my energies are aligned
and going with the flow.

Transitioning into changes
changes that I can't name
changes that I forsake
changes that I proclaim
I hope that I make it
I hope I won't brake
all that I can do is take day it by day

What is life without mistakes,
distractions or derailments?
we live and learn
allow time to take its turn
everything has a purpose
be it a blessing or a curse
we embrace the good,
but run from the bad
when in reality that's all we ever had.

Sometimes I feel like a child
Sometimes I feel like a rockstar
Sometimes I feel like a supermodel
Sometimes I feel like an actress
Sometimes I feel like an activist
Sometimes I feel like a lazy ass
Sometimes I feel like crying
Sometimes I feel nervous
Sometimes I live in a fantasy
Sometimes I want to run far away
but all of the time I feel GOD.

Peace be upon any man that has ever loved me
and peace be upon any man
that has ever wronged me
regardless if one was my friend or my
enemy, they were all my teachers.

Guide me father, be with me mother, help me bother, comfort me sister, love, me.

I love the power black holds
aesthetically, I really love everything
about being black
I love the controversy my skin causes
I love the way my skin glistens in the sun
I love how the glow in my skin is so
powerful that it radiates an entire room
I love how dense and textured my hair is
I love how voluptuous and curvy I am
I love how exotic my eyes look
I love how my brown skin enhances
my pearly white smile
I love how full my lips are and how
high my cheek bones sit
I love how proportionate my body is
I love how my narrow waist and jiggly
thighs complement each other
I love how firm my legs are
I love how my tits are not perfectly
perky but soft as cotton
I love how my stretch marks
camouflage with my brown skin
I love how my height and skin tone
makes me a walking form of art
I love how natural I am that it makes look surreal
I love how my tongue speaks with an accent
I love that I can look delicate
and strong simultaneously
Last but not least I simply love my
black ass when it's flat or fat
I literally love every centimeter of my body
I'm so grateful to my ancestors for my brown skin.

Young black woman this world is yours!
don't be afraid to be the center of attention
embrace your glistening melanin
walk into any space and light it up
and when you find a great support system
stick to it, it'll make you shine more.

Look at you smiling
looking all delighted
since you let go of your fears and
you're no longer frightened.

Time
I have to make better use of it
I'm always abusing it
always making excuses because of it.

No time to dwell,
yet all I do is ponder
of what ifs and how can
only think about right now
that's what they say
but how can I?
when right now feels like forever
I've got a baby to feed
goals to achieve
habits that need to be deceased
and right now just feels like time is passing by
so what do I do?
just breathe
pray
and hope
for a better today
a better tomorrow
a better next week
next month and next year
but why can't I be great every day?
for example
when I plan a vacation, I always
know it'll turn out good
I give myself no space to think of what
could go wrong or if it would
instead I anticipate the vacation
and make the best of it
so what is stopping me from letting
everyday feel like a vacation?
so many things go on in my head
at times I wish I could press pause
I shift my focus from one thing to the next

I get distracted
I find humor and beauty
sadness and displeasure
encouragement and strength
to go on each day.
but it feels like a task
when I know it should not
balance
that's all I have
that's all I need
that's all I want
because time is of the essence
and I have none to spare and none to waste
every second matters
every minute I learn and grow wiser
every day I become stronger
I know that the sun will shine its grace on me
and I know that when sun sets its
footprints against the sky
and the stars begin to shine I'll
be among them too
I know because the wind propels
me to keep going
the trees, plants, and leaves taught me that
everyone and everything has their season
one season is meant for shedding dead weight
and things that no longer serve a purpose
another season is for remaining naked
and bare, vulnerable and uncertain
of what the future will bring
the next season is for growth
the final season is for blossoming and flourishing
and somehow, I feel like I'm in all
four seasons all at once
so what do I do?
I find beauty in the mixture and chaos

I find faith in the sun
I find hope in the air
and comfort in the rain
I try to make the best of it
most days I conquer feeling grateful
but some days I feel defeated
especially in the winter, when I'm naked
and bare, exposed, and vulnerable
so I find solace in hibernating, big comfy
sweaters, and sweet chocolates
a lot of candles and excessive
heat from the furnace
this is how I spend my days
my time.

I'm tired and inspired right now
I want to go to sleep
everyone around me is asleep
I want to dig deep
and discover more treasures
gain pleasures
but my inner voice is yelling "help!!!"
she can't do it all at once
she can do it one at a time though
work on today and the rest will follow
everything will be alright
there's no need to stress and
use all of your might
relax and give yourself more time
it could all be so perfect
but instead it just is what it is
Thank you, angel guides
for continuously showing me signs
soon it'll be showtime
I'll be ready
because I am steady
in faith
love
light
hope
and positivity.

Flourishing into another level
positive level
bigger level
centered level
my level
higher level
better level
happy level
love level, the ultimate level.

How does man suffer and smile simultaneously?
could it be the scorching sun melting
away agonies caused by poverty?
maybe it's the sounds of the drums,
apala, juju, Fuji, and afrobeats
that spreads positive melodies
perhaps it's the strong sense of pride, confident
demeanor, resilient attitude, and endless
gratitude that enables the people of Nigeria
to triumph unsurmountable tragedies
Lagos, Nigeria is one of the fastest
growing mega cities in the world
it's no wonder why the streets overflow
filled with hustlers who have
mastered the art of cajoling
while the notorious government
is being inglorious
people remain hopeful and victorious
with a population over 180 million,
more than 300 tribes
and 580 languages spoken
still a lack of unity and success
class, tribalism, and religion divide
the country's togetherness
the poor are oppressed
while the wealthy progress
nevertheless, they're all blessed
man must eat,
man must give praise,
and man must celebrate
to survive in Nigeria
the soil is fertile
but the conditions are brutal
its natural resources are futile
the place is surrounded by water
yet families starve of hunger

the country is commingled in
peace and calamity
evil and happiness
vodoo and vanity
talent and insanity
riches and poverty
even if they lack, some way,
somehow, they will find a way
regardless of any stipulations, class, or criteria
there's a cry for less corruption
and more devotion
equal education and true emancipation
elevation for the most profound black nation
in a land filled with oil, masses of educated
people, and rich culture infiltrating states and
spaces both in and outside of the motherland,
how and when will Nigeria advance to
becoming the ultimate dreamland?

More consciousness
less fear
more light
less darkness
more happiness
less hatefulness.

Strip me of my name and race,
titles, accolades, and clothes
expose my naked soul
and you will a find a heart worth more than gold
to love me is to know me, the soul of me
to know me is to understand me, the soul of me
to understand me is to accept
me, the soul of me.

Take me to a place where
they don't discriminate
show me around where no one frowns
lead me to the road that's good for my soul.

Three words, always take risk
I am just a girl who was not afraid to take a risk,
take a trip out of my mind,
out of my home
and comfort zone,
make a mistake or fail
I will not be tamed nor constrained
rather I am ordained trained and
proclaimed to be great.

I'm all the way up
gravity is propelling me
the clouds are comforting me
the sun is shining on me
the moon is illuminating on me
as God is guiding me.

Time and time again I ask myself why?
why was I born here?
what does the universe want from me?
does the average person think like me?
what is my purpose?
why is my mind so complex?
will I have enough courage?
will I survive?

Lost leader leads the lost
how can that be?
isn't a leader supposed to give direction?
sometimes
a true leader doesn't need
direction only courage
courage to fail and keep going
courage to uplift those who fall
courage to remain resilient
courage to never settle
courage to choose the right battles
because even when a leader is lost,
the leader will use that same courage
to create their own direction.

I have no desire to be a queen
of a monarchy or regime
there's too many democracies
and not enough honesty
I will lead by my frequency
rule in love and positivity
live in happiness
a life of quality,
that evolves consciously,
through the laws of sacred geometry.

On the journey.

Happy
really and truly
for myself and everyone else.

You have to be grounded in who you are
be real with yourself
accept yourself
know yourself
love yourself
and be proud of yourself
once you master that it won't matter
what society thinks of you because
you're living in your reality.

To surrender is more powerful than remaining.

I've been through enough to know that
everything I do has to flow with me
if it's forced, I'm not doing it.

Any day
any way
however you may
be great.

Divinely guided
well protected
innately blessed.

Love hard every chance you get.

You are enough
even in your flaws.

Every time that I look into your eyes
I know I did something right with my life
every time I think of you I begin to smile
you make me so happy I don't know why
I just really appreciate your existence in my life.

Who I was yesterday is not who I am today
who I was yesterday led me to who I am today
but who I am today is not who I was yesterday
in one day everything changed
nothing is the same.

I made better choices than you
but that doesn't mean I'm better than you
maybe I am more fortunate than you
but that doesn't mean I'm
more blessed than you
or that I sin less than you
I've been in higher places than you
but that doesn't mean I'm smarter than you
I may be ahead today
but that doesn't mean you won't
surpass me the next day
If life truly were a race
I would say we all have what it takes
to come in first place.

I saw a woman perform witchcraft
it was magical in fact
the way she moved the crowd
with the sway of her hips
and her soft cherry lips
her presence was sorcery
she put us under a spell
or maybe she was an angel
I can't tell.

I really don't mean to stare at her
because I'll end up comparing myself to her
I just really like the way she's put together
I wonder what her worth is
what is my worth?
is she better than me?
or am I better than her?
man, I really hate it when I do that
I don't know anything about her
I just like the idea of her
the appearance of her
so I'll bask in her
because once she walks away,
I'll never see her again
and just like that the comparisons
come to an end.

Do not compare me
I don't want to be like anyone else
I don't want to be like you, him, or her
I don't want to know what they are all doing
I don't care what they think of me
I love music more than I do people
so what if I'm always alone and act like a weirdo
I would rather stay in isolation and
fall in love with my flaws.
befriend my fears
console my bad habits
stretch out my sins
create more magic
perfect my craft
learn and unlearn
record my discoveries
share my pieces
inspire and be inspired
then do it all over again.

All that I am
because of my mother I am happy
because of my father I am an intellect
because of my husband I am a woman
because of my son I am a creator.

I am totally surrendering to the unknown
I accept the process of the unknown
I have faith that tomorrow will work
itself out for the greater good
I know in my heart I will end
up where I'm meant to
A place that fulfills my heart and purpose
I will not fear or fret over what
is and isn't in my control
I do not fear the unknown because I
know in the end it will be beautiful
Thank you, God
Thank you, angels
Thank you spirit guides
Thank you, ancestors
Thank you, nature
Thank you, air, fire, earth, and water
I am eternally grateful.